Who were the first people?

Phil Roxbee Cox & Struan Reid

Illustrated by Gerald Wood

Designed by Diane Thistlethwaite & Vicki Groombridge

Cover illustration: Inklink Firenze
History consultants: Dr. Nick Merriman & Dr. Anne Millard
Series editor: Jane Chisholm

CONTENTS

Usborne Quicklinks

For links to websites where you can find out lots more about the first people, how they lived and how we know about them, go to the Usborne Quicklinks website at **www.usborne.com/quicklinks** and type in the keywords **starting people**. Please follow the internet safety guidelines displayed at the Usborne Quicklinks website.

Who were the first people?

No one knows for sure, because they lived such a long time ago. Scientists believe humans or human-like creatures have been on Earth for about two million years.

The funny-sounding names are the ones used by scientists. The words are written in a language called Latin.

What did they look like?

A little different from us. Most scientists believe that very early people, animals and plants changed over hundreds of thousands of years. Some types died out, and others gradually changed into modern people, animals and plants. This is called evolution.

This picture shows a few types of near-humans and early humans.

This is when each type first appeared on Earth.

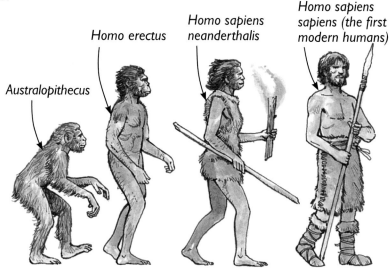

Australopithecus

Homo erectus

Homo sapiens neanderthalis

Homo sapiens sapiens (the first modern humans)

| 3.6 million years ago | 1.8 million years ago | 400,000 years ago | by 130,000 years ago |

What did the first people eat?

They gathered plants and scavenged for meat where they could find it. Later, they hunted animals for food. Scientists call them "hunter-gatherers".

Key:
1 Horse	7 Sabre-toothed cat	12 Homo habilis	18 Phrotherium
2 Wolf	8 Woolly rhino	13 Megaloceros	19 Bat
3 Farmer	9 Macrauchenia	14 Sthenurus	20 Baluchitherium
4 Goat	10 Mammoth	15 Glyptodon	21 Arsinoitherium
5 Giant sloth	11 Homo sapiens	16 Diatryma	22 Pachyrukhos
6 Teratornis		17 Ape	23 Basilosaurus

These animals are walking, swimming or flying along a "time line" in groups. The farther to the right their group is, the farther back in time they are. Look at the key above to find out what they were called.

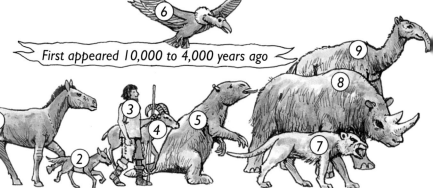

First appeared 10,000 to 4,000 years ago

What does "prehistoric" mean?

"Before history". This was the time before people left any books or writings behind. Prehistory lasted for millions of years. It's much longer than history.

This is an example of some of the earliest writing, which was invented about 5,000 years ago.

How do we know anything about prehistoric people?

Only through the hard work of archeologists. These are people who seek out, dig up and study very old objects and remains.

This object was found by archeologists. What was it? A knife? A comb?

Stone spearhead. The wooden shaft will rot away over time.

This prehistoric boy is learning to make spears by watching his big brother.

By comparing it with earlier finds, and studying things near it, archeologists realized the object on the left was a spearhead.

First appeared 2 million to 54 million years ago

First appeared 4,000 to 2 million years ago

There are more of us on the next page.

Where in the world did they live?

All over the place. Our very earliest ancestors came from Africa. Between 200,000 and 55,000 years ago, different groups started to settle in the Middle East and beyond, reaching Europe and spreading across Asia and into America.

Of course, these places didn't have these names then. There were no such things as countries.

How did they reach these places?

They walked. In fact, hunter-gatherers walked just about everywhere.

A group of them might have walked a few miles and settled in a new place. When their children grew up, this new generation might then move on a few more miles.

A boat made from a tree trunk.

This woman has sore feet.

This baby is enjoying the ride.

This group of prehistoric people has been on the move for months without bumping into anyone else.

How many people were there in prehistoric times?

There were probably only twenty or thirty thousand of the first "true" human beings in the whole world. (Scientists call them *Homo sapiens sapiens*.)

This may sound like quite a crowd, but today there are over seven billion people on the planet.

First appeared 54 million to 135 million years ago

Were they stupid?

Certainly not. Today, people build on and improve ideas, inventions and discoveries made by people from earlier times. The earliest people had to find out everything for themselves.

How big were their brains?

The more advanced our ancestors became, the bigger brains they had. We know this because the fossils of the skulls of very early people are smaller than later human skulls.

This fossilized skull was once on the neck of an early man. There wasn't much room for his brain in this skull.

Brains were inside this part.

This is an early Homo sapiens skull. The domed area on top had room for a much bigger brain inside it.

This is the skull of one of the first true humans. You can see that the skull is bigger still to fit her larger brain.

This is the end of the "time line" that started at the bottom of page 2. It has taken us right back through time to some of the earliest sea creatures. The names of the animals on these two pages are in the yellow box.

Key

1 Coryphodon	11 Archaeopteryx	22 Crinoid (sea lily)
2 Ectoconos	12 Compsognathus	23 Dimetrodon
3 Oxyaena	13 Turrilites	24 Millerosaurus
4 Uintatherium	14 Corythosaurus	25 Cockroach
5 Coelacanth	15 Dimorphodon	26 Ichthyostega
6 Hyracotherium	16 Diplodocus	27 Cystoid
7 Pteranodon	17 Saltoposuchus	28 Stelleroid
8 Plesiosaurus	18 Ichthyosaurus	29 Eurypterid (sea scorpion)
9 Tyrannosaurus rex	19 Stegosaurus	30 Trilobite
10 Triceratops	20 Ammonite	
	21 Meganeura	

First appeared 135 million to 225 million years ago

First appeared 225 million to 550 million years ago

5

What did they look like?

No one knows for sure. Our earliest ancestors didn't paint detailed pictures of each other, or take photographs, so we have very few clues. Most ideas of what they looked like come from studying their remains.

This tiny carving of a person's head is over 25,000 years old.

Were they smaller than us?

Not really. People used to think so because of an early *Homo sapiens* man's skeleton. It was later realized that he wasn't "typical" at all. He had an illness called arthritis, which made him hunched up, so that he looked smaller!

Did they really dress like Tarzan?

No. The first people lived at a time we call the Ice Age. It not only sounds very cold, it *was* very cold.

Skimpy loin cloths, like Tarzan's, wouldn't have kept them warm enough.

This early Homo sapiens is only slightly shorter than the much more modern man standing behind him.

This scene shows some of our early ancestors, back from a cold day's hunting and gathering.

This boy wants his supper.

Animal fur

Harpoon for spearing fish

It is cold outside, so this fire is needed to keep them warm.

Shells for decoration

Clothes made from animal skins

This girl will go hunting too when she is a little older.

6 *Like all the scenes in this book, this one is based on archeologists' ideas of what life was like in the past.*

Did they bother to cut their hair?

Probably. Carvings of heads have been found, showing people with quite fancy hairstyles.

How often they washed their hair is another matter.

These carvings show two very different hairstyles.

What did they make necklaces out of?

All sorts of things, but mainly fossils, shells, pebbles and animal teeth and bones.

This shell and bone necklace would have been a treasured possession.

Did they wear jewels?

Not precious gems. But they did wear necklaces, pendants and earrings made from other things.

Shell

Bone

These bits and pieces are all the ingredients for a necklace.

Shell earring

This prehistoric comb is made from animal bone.

Did you know?

Only a human's thumb can touch the fingertips of the same hand. (Not even apes can do this.) This is why it's much easier for humans to use tools.

It is easy for this person to pick up a pencil.

The shape of this ape's thumb makes picking things up much harder.

Are archeologists ever fooled?

Yes, they're only human. In 1913, a skull was found at a place called Piltdown in England. It had the head shape of a man, but the jaw shape of an ape.

Archeologists were very excited. 40 years later, it was proved to be a trick. Someone had attached an orangutan's jaw to a human skull!

Human skull

Orangutan's jaw

Did they really live in caves?

Some early people did, but most couldn't. Unlike houses, caves can't be built, and if there weren't any in the area, they made do without.

Those who were lucky enough to find a cave lived near the opening. Inside a cave, it was dark and there was no chimney to let out the smoke and smells.

How do we know all this?

From the work of archeologists who study the remains of our ancestors' homes. You can find out more on pages 30 and 31.

These remains of a prehistoric home have been uncovered by archeologists.

Fireplace

Tools to scrape with

Cooking tools

Animal bones

This shows a settlement of hunter-gatherers.

This reindeer will supply a family with food, clothes and tools.

These men are building a tent. One of them is smiling because it will be his new home.

Branches

All the dead animals' flesh is being scraped off the skins so they can be used for clothes.

A bump on the head

Animal skins for the walls

Firewood

Did they have wallpaper?

No, they didn't have any kind of paper. But they did sometimes paint pictures on cave walls. These were usually in the difficult-to-get-to inner parts of the caves, where people didn't actually live. They were often pictures of the animals they hunted.

What are these animals?

This copy of cave paintings shows two animals. Do you know what type of animals they are supposed to be?

What were these inner caves for?

Special occasions. They were probably seen as magical places – doors to another world. People think that they were used by hunters for special ceremonies.

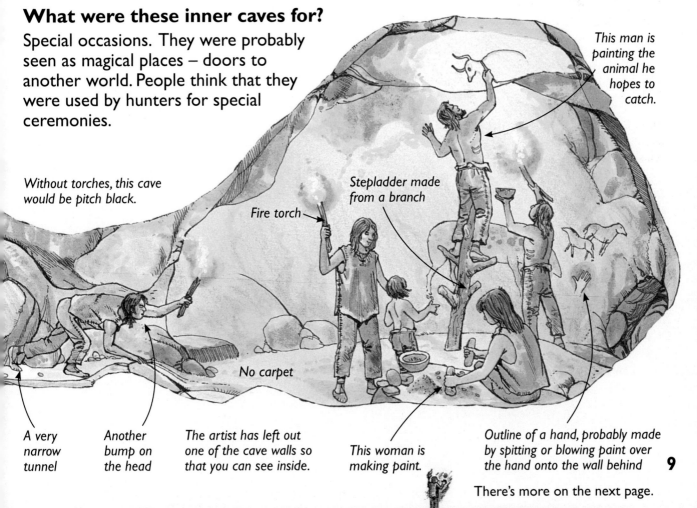

This man is painting the animal he hopes to catch.

Without torches, this cave would be pitch black.

Stepladder made from a branch

Fire torch

No carpet

A very narrow tunnel

Another bump on the head

The artist has left out one of the cave walls so that you can see inside.

This woman is making paint.

Outline of a hand, probably made by spitting or blowing paint over the hand onto the wall behind

9

There's more on the next page.

If they didn't live in caves, where did they live?

Hunter-gatherers built small tent-shaped homes like the ones below. They used sticks, grass, skin and bones. Often, these tents were packed full of people.

Shelters like this one were built about 400,000 years ago. They were made from thin branches and bundles of twigs.

The walls of this house are made out of grass covered with mud. This makes it warm and waterproof inside.

Mammoth bones are the main ingredients for this home. You can see a more detailed picture on page 15.

This is a very simple home. It is made of branches and animal skins. It'll need a few more skins on it to keep the rain out.

How did they keep warm?

With plenty of people crammed into very small houses, the heat from everyone's bodies probably helped. Even so, most prehistoric houses would have been pretty cold. In colder places, some people made fires inside their homes. Clothes kept them warm too!

This group of people in the scene below are hunter-gatherers. They have set up home by a river for a few months. When the weather gets colder, they will be moving on.

Walls made from mammoth hide and other animal skins

Heavy stones hold skins in place.

This hole hasn't been made by a wild animal, but by the artist. This is so that you can see the fire inside the house.

Did they live in towns?

Not for thousands of years. People only began to settle down about 11,000 years ago. Although hunter-gatherers put up their houses in groups, they still moved from place to place.

Did they keep pets?

No. In fact, very early hunter-gatherers would have killed any animal they came across. Then eaten it. Later, they must have realized that dogs could help them hunt.

A stick

The father and mother of these puppies go hunting with the father and mother of this girl.

Food was too precious to share with animals which did not earn it. Even very early farmers, 11,000 years ago, kept animals as workers and not as lazy pets.

Mammoth hide is too tough for making clothes, but it's very good for tents.

Returning hunters

A happy wave

Someone's supper

This woman is building a fire.

This man is trying to fish.

Tool-making

Animal skin pegged out to dry

Firewood

This boy will have a nasty cold by morning.

This man is cleaning animal blood off his shirt.

Did they hunt dinosaurs?

No, no, no and no again. They were as likely to see a dinosaur wandering around then as we are today.

Dinosaurs died out about 62 million years *before* the first people walked on the Earth. They wouldn't even have known what dinosaurs were.

So what did they eat?

Hunter-gatherers ate wild plants, nuts, fruit, fish, shellfish and any animals they could catch and kill.

Exactly what they ate depended on where in the world they lived.

These people are collecting shellfish off the rocks in the shallow water.

Her job is to open the shells.

This prehistoric cave painting shows a hunter using his (or her) bow and arrow to kill a reindeer.

How did they hunt?

On foot, and with their bare hands to begin with. Later, spears were invented. Then, hundreds of thousands of years after that, they hunted with bows and arrows.

Did they go fishing?

Yes, but not with fishing rods and lines. They would have used their hands, spears and, later, nets.

Did they eat chocolate?

No, but they probably liked sweet-tasting things. There was no sugar, but honey made by wild bees would have been popular.

This ancient picture shows a woman climbing a tree to reach honey in a beehive.

Harpoon

Spearheads

How do we know what they ate?

By studying the seeds and animal bones they left behind which archeologists have found.

What sort of weapons did they use?

All sorts. (You'll find some examples on pages 17 and 18.) Spears were usually thrown to kill the animal. Knives and axes were used to cut up the meat.

This man is pretending to make a bone tool. He is really about to have a nap.

Once an animal is killed, it is put to good use. Its flesh is eaten, its skin worn, and its bones used for tools.

Meat is cooked to make it more tasty and less chewy.

This person is talking about the day's hunt.

Were any of our early ancestors vegetarians?

Not if they could help it. People would have eaten whatever they could find, and meat was important for protein. Vegetables and other plants were harder to find in the winter, too.

Eggs

Dandelions

Nuts

Did you know?

Some rubbery tree resin was found in the mouth of a 9,000 year old teenager. Archeologists think he was using it as chewing gum. Plants were also used as medicines.

Catmint was supposed to make colds better.

Rue might have been used to cure headaches.

There's more on the next page.

What were mammoths?

Huge animals, hunted by our ancestors. They were a type of elephant with long, curvy tusks. Mammoths used their tusks to clear away snow and dig up plants to eat. Their remains have been found from Canada to Russia and across Northern Europe. Mammoths were very woolly.

Why were they so woolly?

They lived in the Ice Age. Unlike elephants today (which live in the warm climates of Africa and India), mammoths needed their long, thick hair and layers of fat to keep warm.

Hunters sneak up behind a large male mammoth. The tips of their spears are long and sharp to slice through the animal's woolly coat.

Were there other woolly animals?

Yes, plenty. These included a kind of woolly rhinoceros.

This is a woolly rhinoceros. You can tell it is, because it looks just like a rhinoceros but has hair.

This mammoth has just heard the hunters coming and is about to make his getaway.

Tusk

What did mammoths taste like?

Mammoth, of course! This probably tasted rather like an elephant (whatever that's like). Our ancestors would have cooked it and not eaten it raw.

Ice Age ice and snow

Were mammoths only hunted for food?

No. Different parts of a mammoth were used for an amazing number of different things. In fact, some of our ancestors actually lived in houses built out of mammoths!

This scene shows a house made from mammoth tusks and bones.

A row of mammoth skulls.

These tusks make a good archway.

Happy hunters

Firewood is very important in such a cold climate.

Animal skin walls

Did you know?

The last mammoths died over 10,000 years ago. But a few mammoths' bodies have been found frozen in huge blocks of ice in a very cold place called Siberia, in northern Russia.

They were so cold that they didn't rot away.

This picture shows two Russians finding a frozen mammoth.

15

What tools did they use?

All sorts. Hunter-gatherers went after the same food as many animals. They needed weapons to help them get to this food first.

The more people learned, the more types of weapons and tools were invented.

What tools did they use to make the very first tools?

Good question! The very, very first "tools" would have been *found* not made. For example, a small rock could be used as a hammer.

This man is using a deer's antler to dig a hole.

These branches will be used to make weapons.

Chipping a piece of stone to make tools

This girl is making holes in the skin to sew through later.

Tools are used to scrape these animal skins clean.

How did they make a stone blade?

A type of stone called flint was best for this. It could be chipped into shapes and given a sharp edge.

A piece of flint was given a flat top by hitting it with another stone. This piece is known as the core.

The edge of the core was struck with a bone hammer. This sliced off thin flakes of flint.

These thin flakes were then shaped and sharpened, by carefully chipping the edges with a bone hammer.

Did they really carry big wooden clubs?

A large piece of wood might have been useful to use as a club, but our ancestors had far better weapons. They hunted with spears tipped with points of flint, bone, or even just sharpened wood.

This man is making arrows. They are a new idea.

Bird feathers

These hunters are pleased with their new spears.

Cutting up meat

Did you know?

About 10,000 years ago in the Middle East, early farmers invented a useful new tool called a sickle. A piece of wood or bone was carved into a curve, and slices of sharpened flint were set into the sides to make a blade. It cut through crops quickly.

Can you tell...

...where these Stone Age tools (and parts of tools) appear in the main pictures on these pages, and what they were used for?

An arrowhead

A perforator

A harpoon head

A bone sickle with flint edges

A knife

17

There's more on the next page.

Did they only use weapons made of wood and stone?

For a long time, yes. Then, 6,000 years ago, they discovered metals. The first metals used by early people were copper and gold. Copper was used for making weapons, and gold for decoration.

These two are blowing on the fire to keep the flames hot. It makes them hot too.

Vessel full of hot melted bronze

Why wasn't gold used for making weapons?

Because a gold arrowhead would have bent! It was too soft. Copper was harder, but would become blunt as it was used. Later, a stronger metal was made from copper and tin. It was called bronze, and was turned into everything from swords to pins and knives.

This boy is tying the new metal spearheads to the shafts. He likes this job.

Part of a cast for making large pins for clothes

Why was bronze a good metal to use?

Because it is very strong but easy to shape. This was done by heating it up until it melted and became a liquid. The liquid was then poured into casts and left to cool into solid shapes.

Pot

Sword

Axe head

Clothes pins

All of these objects, on the left, are made of bronze. They were made by early farmers, using casts.

How did they make most pots?

From clay. The first clay pots were made about 10,000 years ago. They were baked in an open fire to harden them. Later on, special ovens, called kilns, were built to make hotter fires for hardening pots.

Water containers

Cooking pot

Cook with backache

This is a kiln, a special kind of oven for hardening clay pots.

Frightened mouse

These prehistoric pots have been decorated in very different ways.

Can pots tell us about ancient people?

Yes. Where the pots were found, what they look like and what they were used for all help to build up a picture of everyday life of the time.

Did they have any machines?

A very simple machine, called a loom, was invented about 11,000 years ago. It was used to weave sheep's and goat's wool into cloth.
    Hunter-gatherers didn't have machines.

Loom

How can I make a prehistoric pot?

You can't, without going back in time. But you could try making a pot in the same sort of way our ancestors did.

Roll some model-making clay into a ball. Press both thumbs into the middle. Then use your fingers to pull up the sides, as shown below.

Another prehistoric pot was the coil pot. You can make a copy of this type by rolling out long thin "snakes" of clay. Then coil each one into a ring, one on top of the other.

Once you have done that, use your fingers to smooth down the sides and make a pattern.

Simple items like these can be used to add patterns.

Why was fire so important?

Because it had so many uses. Our earliest ancestors were probably frightened of fire. But, about 500,000 years ago, they realized that fire could be used for heat, light, cooking and protection.

How did they make fire?

Probably by the simplest method there is: banging two stones together to make a spark. A little later, they probably started rubbing pieces of wood to create a flame.

Drill stick

Hearth stick

The tip of this drill stick is rubbed against the hearth stick to make a flame.

Hundreds of thousands of years ago, hunters like these might have used flaming torches to set fire to grassland and force frightened animals to run into marshy ground.

Once the animals were stuck in the marsh, the hunters could surround them and attack.

These hunters need to know what they are doing. If the fire gets too large, they have no way of controlling it.

This man is in charge.

The seeds from these grasses can also be eaten.

How did they know there was fire before they knew how to make it?

Good question! The answer is that fire occurs naturally, and our ancestors would have seen it. For example, lightning hitting a tree or dry grass can cause a fire.

The tusks will be turned into tools.

The skin will be used to make tents.

The meat will be eaten.

Marshland

Did you know?

In China, there is a cave full of huge piles of 460,000 year-old ash. Archeologists believe that the fires in the cave were never put out. These early people probably didn't know how to make their own flame.

How was fire so useful?

Its warmth meant that people could move to colder areas. Its light meant that people could stay up later, or go farther into dark caves. Fire also frightened away dangerous animals.

Later, it was used for cooking, and to smoke meat and fish. Cooked meat tastes better and can be kept longer than raw meat. Smoked meat can be kept longer still.

These children are busy cooking. Cooking is one of the things that makes people different from other animals.

How did they understand each other?

In many different ways. The words we speak, read and write have taken thousands of years to turn into what they are today. Our earliest ancestors had to make up everything from nothing.

This handprint was found by a painting on a cave wall. Many people left their handprints in paintings. We're not sure exactly why.

How did people first talk to each other?

Nobody knows exactly. Our earliest ancestors probably used a lot of grunts and made expressions with their faces. Hand signals would also have been very useful.

Bat-eared fox   Tortoise   Hare   Ostrich

These are some of the hand signals still used by an African tribe to mean certain animals.

The story this man is telling is full of useful hunting hints.

As the number of words grew, people probably gathered in groups, like this one, to tell stories.

Nice and warm near the fire

Later, *Homo sapiens* would have developed a proper spoken language. We don't know what it was like, because it was never written down. Writing was only invented about 5,500 years ago.

An early example of keeping a record of something.

Cutting nicks into a bone

Many people in this scene are writing things down. See if you can guess what they are recording.

A nosy goat

Why did people need writing?

Writing was only invented once people had settled down to farm. The more people there were in one place, the harder it was to remember who owned what.

Who invented writing?

No single person or single group of people sat down and said:"Hey, let's invent a written language". Writing first developed in Sumer (now part of Iraq), and in Egypt.

These clay tablets are covered in a very old kind of writing called cuneiform. They are from Sumer, and are about 5,000 years old.

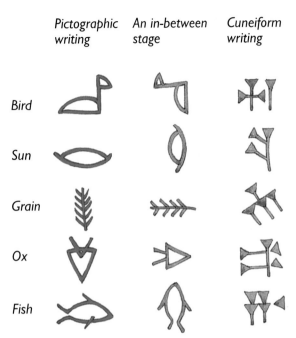

	Pictographic writing	An in-between stage	Cuneiform writing
Bird			
Sun			
Grain			
Ox			
Fish			

The first writing is known as pictographic writing. It used pictures as words. In Sumer, the pictures slowly changed into symbols. Their writing is called cuneiform. "Cuneiform" means wedge-shaped. It was written by pressing a wedge-shaped tip onto clay.

Did they have books?

No. They didn't even have paper to write on. But the remains of an archive built by early farmers was found in a place called Ebla, in what is now Syria.

A chunky librarian hard at work

Clay tablet "books"

Over 1,900 clay tablets such as these were found.

Part of the Ebla archive might have looked like this.

Are picture symbols still used today?

Yes. This symbol is still used all over the world. Do you know what it means?

If not, find out on page 32.

How did they get around?

Most of the time, they walked – a lot. Hunter-gatherers needed to travel around to find food and shelter. They followed animals when they were hunting, and moved to different places in different seasons.

Did they have roads?

Our earliest ancestors didn't, but once they had begun to settle in places, they probably used the same routes to travel between them. By around 6,000 years ago, wooden trackways were sometimes built across marshy ground.

This group has been on the move for days. They are carrying everything they own.

A quick bite to eat

This girl is annoying her mother.

Meat for the next week

These children are playing at hunting.

What if it snowed?

They'd stay at home if they could. It would have been too cold, too difficult and too tiring for weaker members of the family to go far in such bad weather.
   Some people probably *had* to go out to find food.

An early skier dressed for action

Did they ride horses?

Not hunter-gatherers. Horses probably weren't tamed until at least 6000 years ago. Even then, people were more likely to eat them, or use them to pull loads, rather than ride them.

Experts are still puzzling over this horse's head carving. It was carved by hunter-gatherers, but it looks as though it is wearing a harness to be ridden.

Did they use boats?

Yes, from about 55,000 years ago. At first, boats were probably just tree trunks. By about 6,000 years ago, there were some proper sailing ships.

This boat is made from half a log, with the wood hollowed out of the middle.

Paddle

Fishing spear

An unfortunate fish

This picture on this pot is of an early ship. The pot is almost 6,000 years old and was made in Egypt.

Cabins

Oars

How did they move heavy things without trucks?

With difficulty! When they wanted to shift things, such as a rock, they made rollers out of tree trunks.

Once the rock had rolled off a roller, the roller could then be put in front of it and used again.

This is certainly a heavy thing! It's a stone for a temple.

These people have turned around to heave this stone uphill.

Didn't they have carts?

Not for a long time. And for a very good reason. No one had invented the wheel until almost 5,500 years ago.

The first carts had solid wheels made from circles of wood cut from tree trunks. Later, metal rims were added to them to make them stronger.

Wooden rollers

Why was the wheel important?

Because people could move faster, and take more with them. For example, a donkey can carry three times as much in a cart as it can on its back.

This clay model of an Indian cart was made about 5,500 years ago.

How did farming change their lives?

Completely and utterly. When farming started about 11,000 years ago, people began to settle down. Unlike hunter-gatherers, early farmers could stay in one place. In time, real villages began to grow up.

Did they milk cows?

Not to begin with. Cows were just used for meat. Goats' milk was drunk long before cows' milk. After about 1,000 years (that's about 10,000 years ago), early farmers began to milk cows.

What animals did they keep?

Sheep and goats, to begin with. These were originally hunted by people of the Middle East, who later became the first farmers. From about 10,000 years ago, pigs and cows were kept too.

Earth for building a new house

Builders busy building

An unsafe-looking ladder

People drying fruit

— This cow is quite happy staying where it is.

This dog is pleased to see its master.

This picture shows what an early Middle Eastern farming settlement might have looked like.

The laziest person on the farm

Which crops did they grow?

Wheat and barley, at first. These were once wild grasses. Farmers would have collected the seeds and planted them. They soon discovered which plants made the best grain.

This person is milking a goat.

In the Middle East, walls and houses were built out of mud bricks.

These people are making pots.

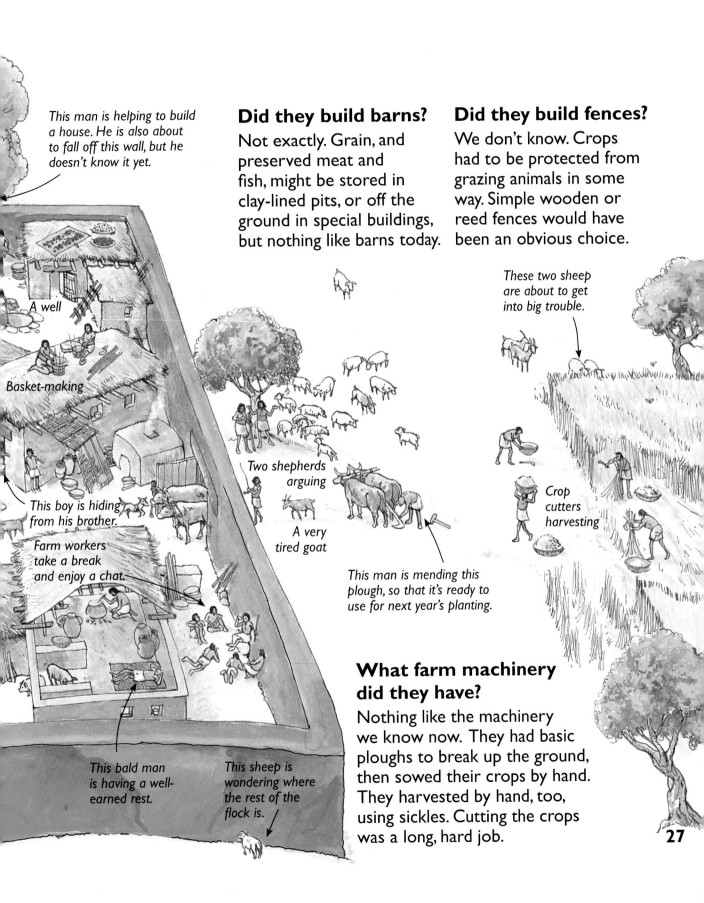

This man is helping to build a house. He is also about to fall off this wall, but he doesn't know it yet.

Did they build barns?

Not exactly. Grain, and preserved meat and fish, might be stored in clay-lined pits, or off the ground in special buildings, but nothing like barns today.

Did they build fences?

We don't know. Crops had to be protected from grazing animals in some way. Simple wooden or reed fences would have been an obvious choice.

A well

Basket-making

This boy is hiding from his brother.

Farm workers take a break and enjoy a chat.

These two sheep are about to get into big trouble.

Two shepherds arguing

A very tired goat

Crop cutters harvesting

This man is mending this plough, so that it's ready to use for next year's planting.

This bald man is having a well-earned rest.

This sheep is wondering where the rest of the flock is.

What farm machinery did they have?

Nothing like the machinery we know now. They had basic ploughs to break up the ground, then sowed their crops by hand. They harvested by hand, too, using sickles. Cutting the crops was a long, hard job.

27

Did they believe in God?

Our ancestors probably believed in many different gods and goddesses. Anything which seemed magic would have been seen as a god – from the Sun and Moon to fire, wind and water.

This is probably not meant to be a pointy hat, but the goddess's hairstyle. She looks pleased with it.

How do we know about their gods?

From the clues archeologists have found. In the Middle East, a number of small stone and clay figures have been discovered with huge staring eyes. Archeologists believe that these are models of some of their early gods.

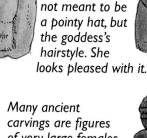

Many ancient carvings are figures of very large females, such as these. Some experts think that these are models of a great Mother Goddess.

This strange-looking figure was made by early people in eastern Europe, who lived by fishing.

A burial is taking place. There is music and dancing from the dead people's friends.

Did our ancestors bury their dead?

Sometimes, but people were also cremated or left in rivers. Early farmers sometimes put piles of earth over the top of the grave, to mark the spot.

This man is in charge.

Simple hollow pipe made from bone

Friends bring presents.

Did they believe in heaven?

It seems so. People were often buried with the tools and weapons they were thought to need on the journey to a new life. Some bodies were also buried with food.

Food, tools, and weapons for their journey to the next life

This man is making plenty of noise with his mammoth's skull drum. He goes to all the funerals.

Did they have ceremonies?

Yes. There is plenty of evidence of religious ceremonies from the time of the early farmers about 10,000 years ago. Archeologists have even found clues to suggest that hunter-gatherers had ceremonies too.

Where did they pray?

At first, deep inside caves and, later, in clearings in woods and forests.

When people began to settle down, the first shrines and temples were built.

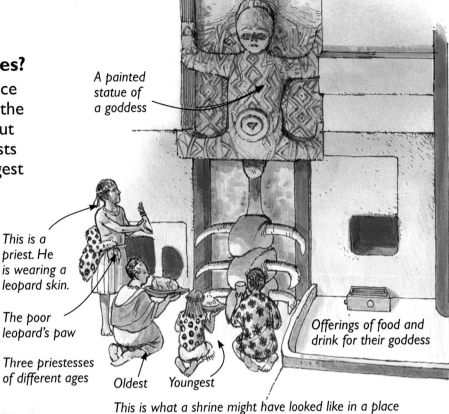

A painted statue of a goddess

This is a priest. He is wearing a leopard skin.

The poor leopard's paw

Three priestesses of different ages

Oldest *Youngest*

Offerings of food and drink for their goddess

This is what a shrine might have looked like in a place called Çatal Hüyük, now in Turkey, 8,000 years ago.

What were the first temples like?

Very different from each other – from rooms over and under the ground in Malta to standing stones and stone cirles in northern Europe.

This is what the temples of Tarxien in Malta might have looked like 5,000 years ago.

Most important temple

Thatched roofs

Stone walls

29

What goes on at an archeological dig?

The word "archeology" means "the study of everything ancient". On a dig, archeologists try to build up an idea of how people lived in the past. They do this from the clues our ancestors left behind.

Archeologists work like detectives, gathering evidence from the remains of pottery, bones, pollen, insects, buildings and whatever else they find.

This man isn't looking where he's going.

A small archeological dig. Here archeologists, students and volunteers work together.

Pickaxes and wheelbarrows are used for shifting soil.

This student has poured rubble on her foot.

This archeologist is very carefully scraping away the soil with a tiny tool.

These human skulls are an exciting find.

Our ancestors didn't live underground, so why do we have to dig to find their homes?

Because soil is made up of the trees and plants which have died and rotted over millions of years. This means that the ground level is much higher today.

These bones have been covered by rotting plants that have then turned into soil.

These people should be working, not having a picnic.

A striped pole. It is called a ranging pole.

What are the striped poles for?

To show how big an object is. For example, if you saw a picture showing a wall and nothing else, you would have no idea of its size. But, with one of these poles in the photographs, you would be able to work out the size of the wall.

These grids are laid on the ground. What is inside the grid is drawn on a chart.

This isn't a tent window. The artist drew the tent like this so that you can see inside.

This woman is the head archeologist. She is in charge and is keeping a record of everything found so far.

The finds are studied here first. (Unless it's raining.)

What is carbon dating?

A way of telling the age of certain remains. Living things, such as plants, animals and people, contain something called carbon-14. When they die, the amount of carbon-14 in them gets less. Experts can measure the amount of it in what they're studying. They can then tell its age.

According to carbon dating, this piece of an ancient carving is thought to be 20,000 years old.

Index

Answers
Page 9.
The animals in the cave painting are supposed to be a horse and a cow.
Page 17.
All the answers are in the pictures and labels. Look carefully!
Page 23.
The symbol is a warning that something is radioactive.

This edition first published in 2015 by Usborne Publishing Ltd, 83-35 Saffron Hill, London EC1N 8RT, England. www.usborne.com